Gemini

Gemini

by

Arthur Turfa

BROAD
RIVER
BOOKS

GEMINI

Copyright 2018 by Arthur Turfa.

All rights reserved.

Printed in the United States of America. No parts of the book may be reproduced in any manner without written permission except in the case of brief quotations embodied in critical articles and reviews.

Library of Congress Number: 2018935657

ISBN: 978-1-942081-17-3

Cover art by Carol Levy

BROAD
RIVER
BOOKS

To Pam, Drew, Amy, Holden, and Carol - who have been with me on the way.

Contents

Prologue to Gemini
3

Reflections on Antietam
5

Puerto Rico Post-Hurricane Maria
7

Conversation on the Steps of the Reserve Unit
8

Golden State Reverie
9

The Shenandoah Valley in Morning Light
11

New River Valley 2017
12

Rivers
13

The Poem Lorca Never Wrote
14

Thoughts on Chagall's Blue Violinist
15

From a Prompt
17

Tuesdays in the 11th Floor Chapel
18

Jimmy
19

Scholarly Mercenaries
21

Looking Ahead and Around – for JMS
23

The Garland
24

The Poet's Poet
25

The Light of Creativity
27

Early Encounter
29

The Fields at Eventide
31

The Afterglow
32

Aubade
33

From Deepest Woods
34

In Timeless Light
35

Conclusion
37

Acknowledgements
41

About the Author
43

Whitman, Song of Myself: Do I contradict myself?
Very well, then, I contradict myself; I am large -- I contain multitudes."

Prologue to Gemini

Maybe because I am a Gemini

have I found myself between two somethings:

English and German, opposite ends of

Pennsylvania, ecumenical views,

Atlantic and Pacific coasts, two nations,

Wahlberliner und Wahlunterfranke,

academic departments, pursuing

bi-vocational careers long before

such blending ceased to appear scandalous

to those not attuned to duality.

Nowadays such pairings appearing in

confusion over headlines and sound bites,

the unavoidable cacophonies

between news and fake news: Babel's Tower

casting a shadow the horizon round.

Release comes to me in creative realms,

in Castalia or in the morning

where inspiration makes everything new.

Like the albatross whose wings are restrained

but surrounding pressures, I yearn to break

free and soar to that place I can see

sun and moon at the same time, where both sides

of the coin meld perfectly into one

and the counterpoint plays in unison.

Rilke, Sonnets to Orpheus, Part One, XII

Bless the spirit that makes connections,
for truly we live in what we imagine.

"Only he whose bright lyre
has sounded in shadows
may, looking onward, restore
his infinite praise.

Reflections on Antietam

Slender fences separate fields:
A wooden lattice extending
over the hills, rolling wave-like
towards the stream connecting the corn
to several groves and the old church .
Occasionally some scattered
farmhouses punctuate the view.

One September afternoon
minie balls and artillery
sliced the air, blood stains covered fields.
Many of the slain left for months
where life was wrenched away from them.

In a war unnecessary
this victory critical for
Emancipation, Antietam
sparked the glimmer of Union hope.

Not far from blood-saturated
fields, newer conflicts have claimed lives:

a cup of trembling among us.

Lincoln's tears water hallowed ground

and mourn for his party, his land.

Puerto Rico Post-Hurricane Maria

When the earth shook in Nicaragua
Roberto Clemente cancelled his plans
and intended to assure that aid would
not be denied to destitute people.
With cargo incorrectly-loaded, his
plane crashed off the coast of his beloved
island, becoming his watery grave.

What millionaire athlete flies to San Juan
or elsewhere on that shattered, sad island?
A barrage of tweets from private gold club
and tossed paper towels belittle
the island and her people.

Conversation on the Steps of the Reserve Unit

Pre-mobilization mayhem on a cold, gray
New Jersey January morning. Senior NCO

wearing a stunned face stammers about
not working in his MOS for two decades.

I recall him snarling in formation a
few months ago about the equation that

being in uniform means WHEN NOT IF
being deployed. Better Soldiers were

sandbox-bound; we were slated for backfill
in Germany. I offer to intercede, being a

chaplain. He shakes his head, then enters
the building. When the plane leaves one

colder night from McGuire, he remains
behind with the rear detachment.

Golden State Reverie

Some places remain with us long after
we leave them. For a time California

was the magnet to my iron, but stronger
forces directed me elsewhere. Now and then

I wonder about things had I returned
as a bachelor, or if my family had gone

there instead of Wilkes-Barre. Joy upon
joy has showered on us all the same.

Every so often though I imagine a cool, clear
Los Angeles night. Jack Webb and Frank Zappa

have a smoke and discuss jazz. Don Van Vliet
paints a landscape while Charles Bukowski

and I discuss literature and decadence over
a round that I have bought. Philip Marlowe

sits at the corner of the bar and moves the
whiskey from the glass to his throat. In a

flash we are walking along the Newport
Back Bay in brilliant sunlight, looking

at the mountains in the distance. Our futures
are hazy like the smog, and soon to separate.

The reverie ends, and I am were I should be.
California Dreaming cannot compete with where

and what the years have rendered to me.
I gaze at the tall pines and am at peace.

The Shenandoah Valley in Morning Light

The soft arms of the field

rise in the morning sun.

Their soft beauty strikes me

as a woman abed, still

in slumber, her mind far away.

Fields extend to the horizon,

tree-crested ridge above

as locks of hair spread out.

If only I could lie in the

dewy meadow, thinking of my true love.

New River Valley 2017

Green hills slip in the sunlight
grassy undulations at times.

Groves stretch into forests leading
to mountaintops that look like an embrace

of welcome. In morning's crisp
coolness, when all is reborn

I contemplate a return to the place
that at times I feel I never should have left.

Then roll floods of memories and
I sense destiny unfolded as it was

intended to be. Knowing that there
are places still welcoming me

sweetens my journey and brings peace
to me now in this sheltering valley.

Rivers

Before the trails, roads and interstates

the rivers flowed under sun and moon.

Now surrounding the city, they

surge seaward, at times they

surge through the streets.

Always-present, outlasting

all who cross over them,

all who play on them.

After all fades, after all is forgotten.

the rivers will flow under sun and moon.

The Poem Lorca Never Wrote

Six days on the sea road,

prow facing westward. For one

a visit, for the other, a new life.

Unequal in age, background and

language, bonds deepened. Did

he yearn to be a father himself?

Adventure reflected in their eyes,

glancing off the waves, shining

as the sun leading them to

New York. The friendship fleeting,

consigned to an unwritten poem

stored in a poet's crowded recollection.

Perhaps later the boy learned of

the cruel fate of the kind man he

knew and looked East once more.

Thoughts on Chagall's Blue Violinist

In a moonlit sky

the violin calls over the village

and even farther away, to distant stars.

A lullaby from a time long ago,

at times sad, at times joyful;

a tune one cannot forget.

Sleep, sleep soundly,

and see what melody the next day

will have for you.

I am in the hands of my insomnia.

Climb up to be the one

to convey to my people longing

a meaning for their life.

Lonely soul lost under

the arching indifferent sky,

you will hear my violin

and be consoled

with my dream without words.

I feel before Kingdom Come

we'll suffer more.

I am the one who fears most

the everlasting curse.

But still, sleep tight my love

Your fiddler on the roof will stay

and sing for you

a song without words.

In a moonlit landscape

Of undulating roofs

the violin voice wafts

penetrating the walls,

It nests in newborn hearts

to carry the tune to the next day

From a Prompt

You and the music flow into one
essence. The notes hover above

and around you, flowing from you,
flowing towards you. For my part

I want to touch the strings and
join in the melody. They vibrate

and burst into a new song. Our
chords are in accord. In this brief

time there is nothing but our song,
each other, this transient harmony

Tuesdays in the 11th Floor Chapel

Riding his bicycle, dressed in second-hand black
the year round, Father Fackler carved time
from the harsh realities of an urban parish
to say Mass for our motley crew of High Church
types seeking solace for half an hour.

Suffering years before the blows of bigots and a
host of other indignities, he combined street smarts
with liturgical precision. Woe to the seminarian
slow to ready the vessels of grace or imprecise
in gesture. Patiently, he taught them all.

Consistency he embodied; he celebrated no
differently in the chapel than at Mt. Calvary
or at any altar. He anchored us in a reality
he now enjoys in its fullness.

Of late when I preside, I pause, reflecting
on him and a growing host of others,
At the verge of eternity I sense their
presence and for a moment, we connect.

Jimmy

In spite of a playground accident
Jimmy found joy in life while
Unable to follow a career path.

Instead he followed a route
Along the highway and
Several secondary roads
Collecting bottles and cans,
An aging man walking
An old bicycle with baskets.
Lunching at the usual places
People kept an eye out for him
As he went on his daily rounds.

One day a teenager texted
While he drove along the highway.
He hit Jimmy and propelled
him 60 feet away and almost
as many days in the hospital.
I haven't seen Jimmy since
Along the side of the highway

Late in the afternoon, walking

Now he spends his time

in a nursing home

carefully coloring page after

page with precision and joy.

Scholarly Mercenary

From high school rooms rented out
at night to community or tech colleges,
with an occasional four-year
campus in the mix, I wander
shoulder bag crammed with
textbooks, papers, flash drive
instead of ammo and field rations.

Contracted from semester to semester,
lured by another check or recertification
points, perhaps more dollars poured
into the Holy Grail of retirement,
on the front lines of education can
we be found around 75% of the time.

No tenure secures us. Some of us have
only these classes. A few seek full-time
status. Not I; my salary suffices.

When the curriculum changes, I change
enough to continue, unwilling to

challenge directly. I am needed, and

say to myself

Vive l'argent! Vive le métier scholaire

Vivle les beaucoup savants mercenaires!

Looking Ahead and Around

– for JMS

Let not tragedy define you, Memories,

even life itself, cannot be wrenched

from you, regardless of past trials.

Embrace, cherish those memories,

receive strength from strangers and

friends alike, from music and poetry

that blend together into compassion

and courage. In this way you will

transcend these days. Those whom you

love, those whom you hold dear will

remain with you. Find solace in those

bonds that cannot ever be rent asunder

The Garland

In the columned vestibule, where garlands
dandled like plumes on exotic birds

between the quartz pillars, glistening in
afternoon sunlight, she waited for him,

extending an arm along the back of a
chair. Upon his entrance he did not

eschew customary greetings, but instead
lifted the lovely limbs to him. She hastened

to his embrace, their lips pressing to
the other's. In a moment a garland broke

and scattered petals lined the marble floor
making it like unto a forest glade, smelling

of pine and moss. She received him warmly
and time stood still, the earth turned no more.

The Poet's Poet

At Castalia is one from
far away, a place that I

have never seen, yet have
longed to know. She

embodies millennia of
treasures, sharing them

with any who wish to learn
from them, She offers all

that she has and gladly
receives all that you would give.

When she departs, Angel, guide
her footsteps, Make her path

easy to walk and gladden
her heart wherever she goes.

When she returns to Arcadia

she brightens all with her being.

The Light of Creativity

In morning freshness, I walked
along Castalia's winding banks.

At the forest's edge, I sensed
the presence of another.. Then

I glanced and saw emerald eyes
reflecting the glory of known worlds.

Around the eyes strands of light
hair mingled with leafy branches.

She stepped onto the dewy meadow,
causing the stream to sing in welcome,

the clear waters filled my soul
with sweet melody and great joy.

She is the sunset, and I am
the sunrise: each of us shining

into the darkness. Our created
light calling others to the light

which is uncreated. We embrace
and bask in that light, in that glow.

Early Encounter

In the hour of just-dawn
dew glistens from the grass.

She walks the meadow's verge,
white gown clinging to her form,

shoulders bare in morning chill,
touched by thick tresses.

When she sees his arrival
her eyes shine like twin suns

rising in the heavens. They kiss
and for an instant the world

fades into shadowy mists.
Shedding her gown, she lies

down. Sweet-smelling grasses
mingle with her hair as he

cushions her back, dewy forearms
embracing her, legs entwined.

Her rising melds with his descending.
Afterwards they lie beside each other,

enveloped in sweet languor that
only lovers lay claim to.

The Fields at Eventide

Shadows from surrounding trees

blend with descending darkness;

the gentle field awaits dawn.

When I pass at eventide,

there remains a lingering

image of Muses dancing

to melodies heard by them

alone. Movements transporting

beauty and bliss to my eyes

as their sweet circle rotates.

The Afterglow

In your purgatory the flames plagued you,
especially in the year of silence.
Did my words deliver any solace
to you as you wandered in the wasteland?
My orisons rising, crashing like waves
against a distant, unresponsive shore.
When you reached the ridge leading to the light,
the downward path proved easier. Once more
you smiled. Healing poured over you in waves
of light. Again you shone with the brightness
of unending sunlight and loving warmth.
The afterglow burst upon me, giving
renewed hope and rejoicing beyond words.
As best I can, give I them expression

Aubade

In early dawn the sunlight shimmers
at the edges of her white gown.

Dewdrops extend from its edges
transformed into prisms of brilliant

colors from spectrum round,
glistening before they vanish.

She hears her name whispered,
resounding in morning stillness

And it is as the ocean roars
or gales slash through the forest.

Seeing him from across the meadow
he leaps the stream to greet her.

They embrace as the sun climbs
higher above the horizon, tenderly

He lays her among the tall sweet grass
whose fragrance rivals the flowers'

Arrayed alongside the curving path.
cradled in his arms, she turns her head,

Smiling as she sweetly opens herself
to his love, his life, his everything.

From Deepest Woods

As you step from deepest woods
may your gaze first fall upon me.

Take my hand and walk with me
across the grassy meadow. Let the

scent of wildflowers sweeten your
soul. Let the sun kiss your shoulders.

Should the meadow end and dark
forest face us, step carefully though it.

If our hands unclasp, I shall hear
your song through the branches

and will seek another glade in
eternally-extending fields on

which you stand shining and
stretch your sweet arms to me.

In Timeless Light

On the ridge resting under the tall pines,
my gaze turns back toward the soft sunset.

Its remaining rays longer, shining on
distant beaches and far-off verdant fields

that I remember more than I can glimpse,
My universe contains several more suns

to gladden my way ahead. Yet I choose
to walk along the ridge a while longer,

so that the image of that one sunset
embeds itself in me as I proceed.

Other suns have set, and more will follow.
Thanks I render for their light, for their love.

When blow cold wintery blasts within my heart,
still it retains the golden day's ardor.

Then I see the fields that last forever,

and behold all of you in timeless light.

Conclusion

At last my two paths have merged into one,
duality coalesced into a single entity.

Beholding sun and moon simultaneously
all I require spread before me.

In wide green fields resplendent in
uncreated light my lyre resounds in

eternal praise to the One who reconciles
every dichotomy, who removed the mists

around my duality, and revealed the harmonies
only a few of us recognized in earlier days.

Around me stand those who sweetened my way,
who shared some of the song, walked some of the path.

On the verge see I on the tree line those
who encouraged me without beholding all

that I would see, their visions becoming mine.
From the ridge looking downward

at those whom I inspired to follow after me
hoping they see me on a far horizon.

I have soared far above the confusions
and the oceans of negativity that engulfed

so many, those who scorned my flight and
remained in comfortable confinement.

Neither contradictions nor opposites were
my duality, now fused into oneness.

Connections now fashioned will remain
unsundered. What was in shadows imagined

bursts into life where visions and reality
flow into never-ending reality.

Point and counterpoint: a fugue echoing through
space and time, each part linked to the other,

the harmonies resonating in unending light

merged into who I have become at last.

Acknowledgements

Thanks to Martha Magenta for her insights on how to begin this book. And to many who were with me as I lived the dualities!

~

Conversations on the Step of the Reserve Unit appeared in the Feb/Mar 2018 issue of *"Blue Streak: A Journal of Military Poetry*

~

Afterglow appeared in the January *Whispers*, January 26, 2018
http://whispersinthewind333.blogspot.com/

About the Author

Arthur Turfa's generation originated the phrase, "What's your sign?" In his case, being a Gemini (and being married to one as well) reflects dualities in his life and careers. Much of his life has been spent between two coasts, continents, languages, and careers. Even within those careers, there have been dualities—civilian/military ministry, several certifications for teaching. In his poetry, the dualities also present themselves.

Currently Turfa teaches at Blythewood High School and Midlands Technical College, and serves as needed in parishes as a supply pastor/priest.

Originally from Pennsylvania, Turfa has lived in several states, as well as Germany, before coming to South Carolina. His family is happy to be in the Midlands. Each of these places, and others as well, find their way into his poetry.

Turfa's previous work includes print and electronic publications nationally and internationally and his books are *Places and Times* 2015, *Accents* 2018, and *Saluda Reflections,* forthcoming in 2018.

www.ingramcontent.com/pod-product-compliance
Lightning Source LLC
Chambersburg PA
CBHW071758080526
44588CB00013B/2291